THE REAL STORY OF JESUS

iBIBLE: The Real Story of Jesus
Copyright © 2023 by RevelationMedia LLC
Published by RevelationMedia LLC
PO BOX 850005
Richardson, Texas 75085-0005

All rights reserved. No part of this publication may be reproduced, distributed, or transmitted in any form or by any means, including photocopy, recording, or other electronic or mechanical methods without the prior written permission of the publisher, except in the case of brief quotations used in noncommercial uses permitted by copyright law.

Images from iBIBLE by RevelationMedia
Author: Steve Cleary
Creative Director: Andrea Wilson
Copy Editor: Lisa Cooper
Graphic Designer: Daphne Keskinidou

Distributed by RevelationMedia [www.RevelationMedia.com]
Printed in U.S.A.
www.i.BIBLE
#iBIBLE
ISBN: 979-8-9871384-4-1

May the story in these pages bring you
closer to **Jesus**, the "way, the truth, and the life."
He calls you by name into a relationship with Him
and promises **eternal life to all who believe**.

In the beginning,
when God created
the heavens and the earth...

...when He created every living creature, great and small, that lives in the seas...

7

...and every variety of winged bird, livestock, creatures that crawl, every beast, and all wildlife, Jesus was there.

9

When God created mankind, male and female, in His own image, and when He told them to be fruitful and multiply, Jesus was there.

Jesus was with God, and He was God, and nothing was created without Him.

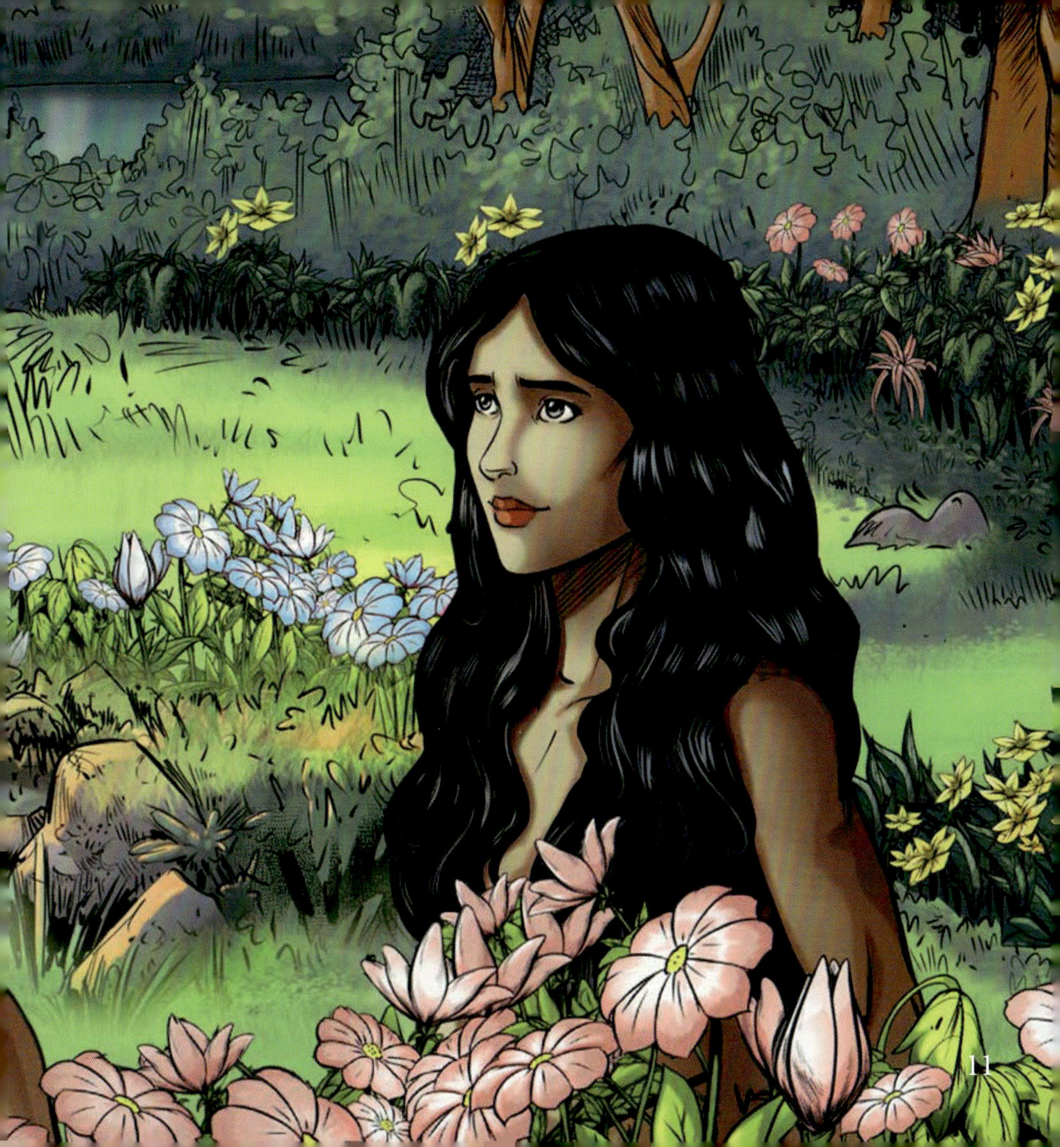

When the first man and woman were deceived by the serpent and disobeyed God...

13

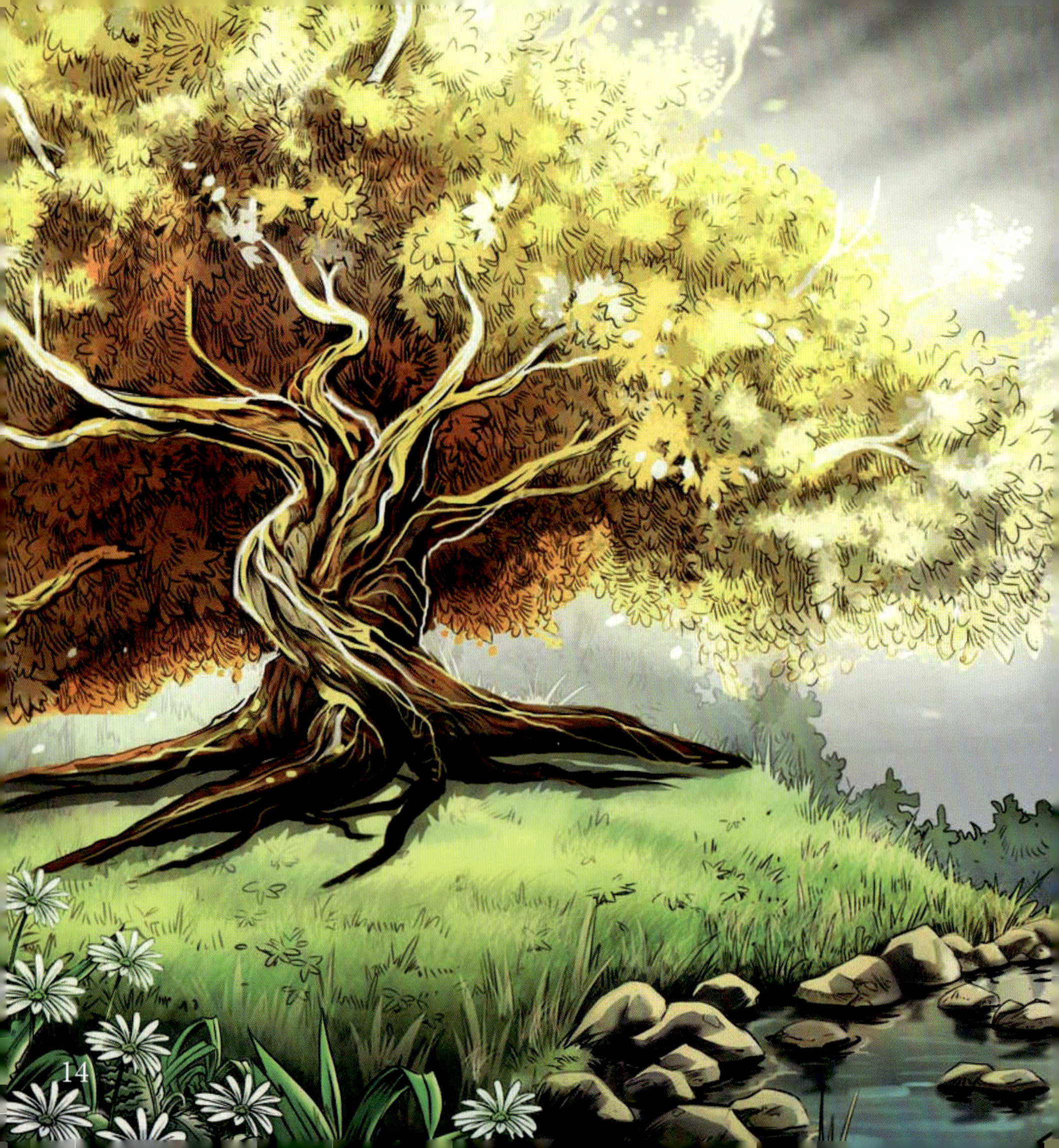

...sin and death entered the world, and mankind was separated from God.

But God promised that one day a Child would be born Who would crush the head of the serpent. This Child would be Jesus.

In time, God made a covenant with a righteous man named Abraham. He promised that Abraham's future Offspring would bless every nation on earth. This Offspring would be Jesus.

17

18

Many years passed, then God spoke through His prophet Isaiah, proclaiming: "A Child will be born of a virgin, and His name shall be called Wonderful Counselor, Mighty God, Everlasting Father, and Prince of Peace."

At the appointed time, an angel named Gabriel visited a virgin named Mary and told her that she would be with child through the power of the Holy Spirit. The Child would be called the Son of God.

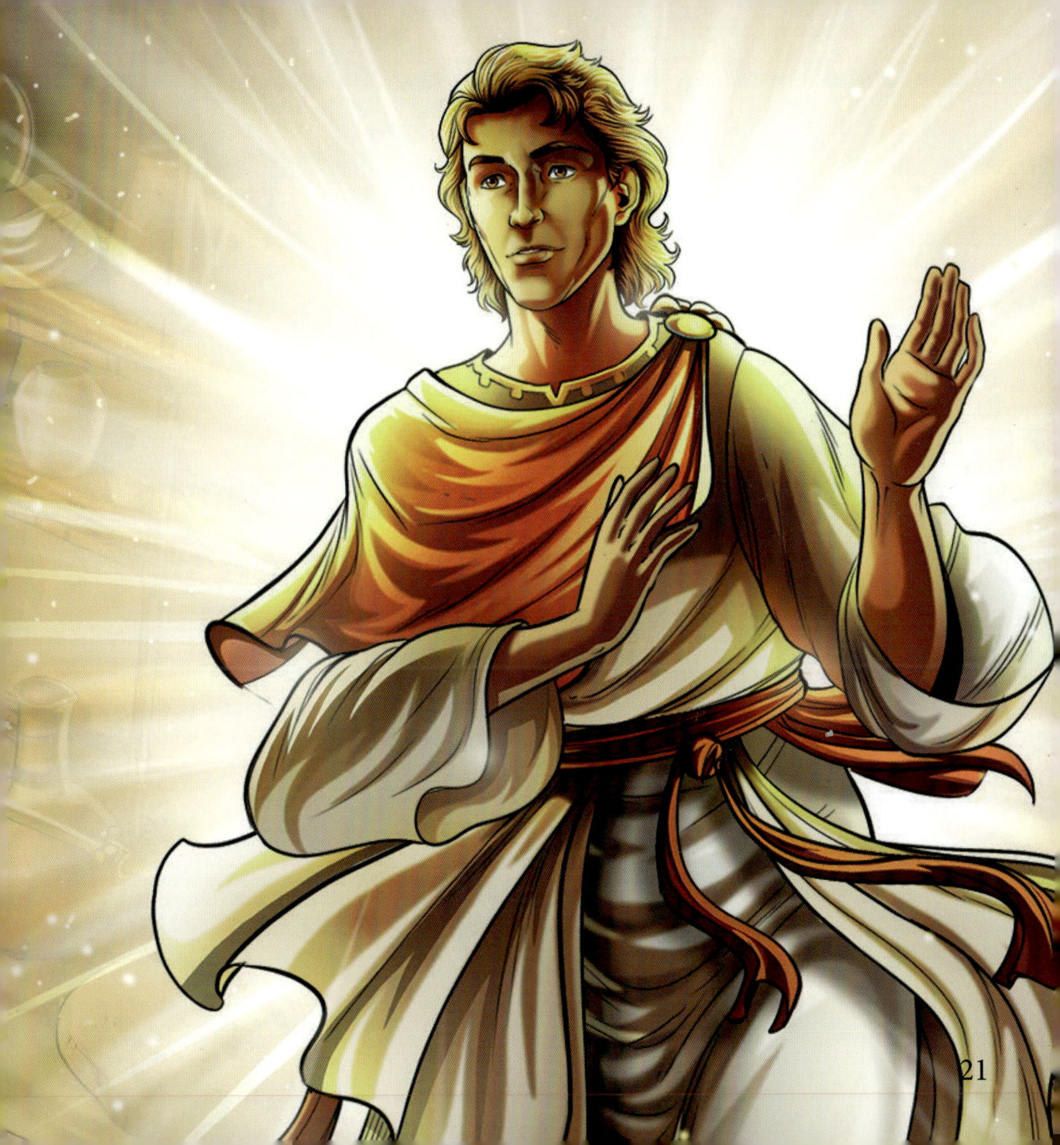

Mary did give birth to the Child, and she named Him Jesus, as the angel had instructed.

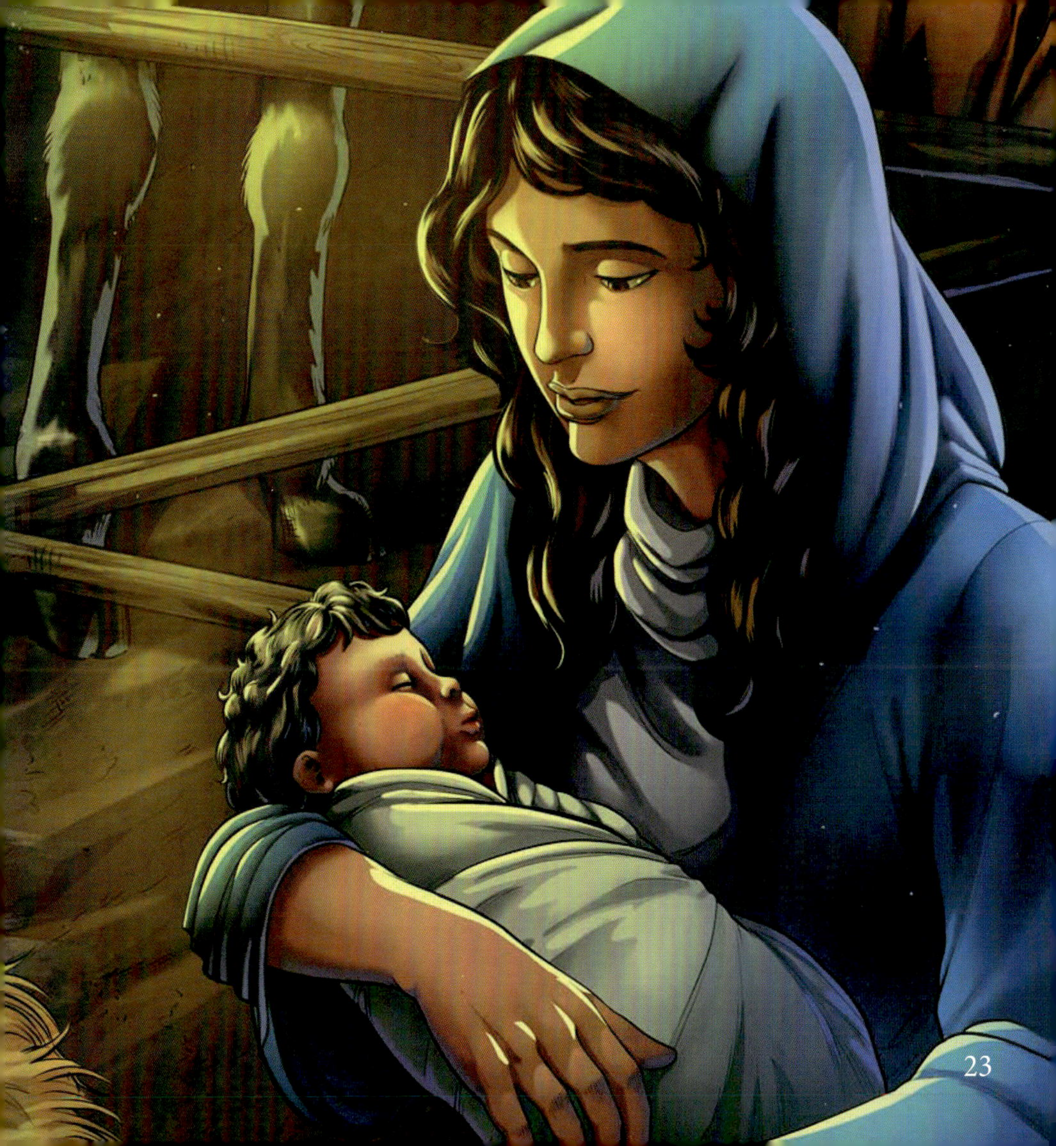

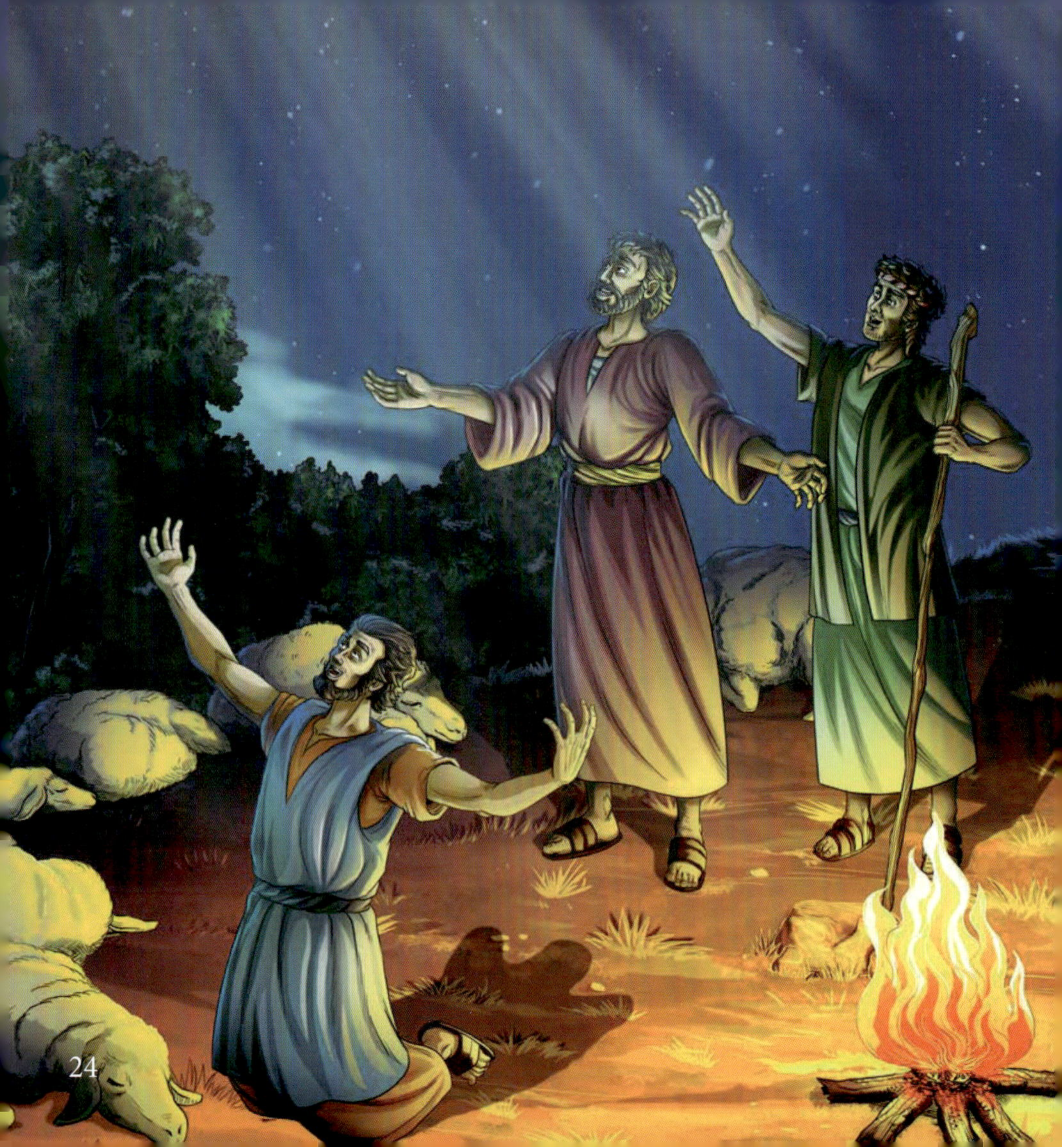

An angel also appeared to shepherds who were tending their flocks by night and told them that in Bethlehem, a Savior had been born.

The shepherds would find the Child wrapped in swaddling clothes, lying in a manger.

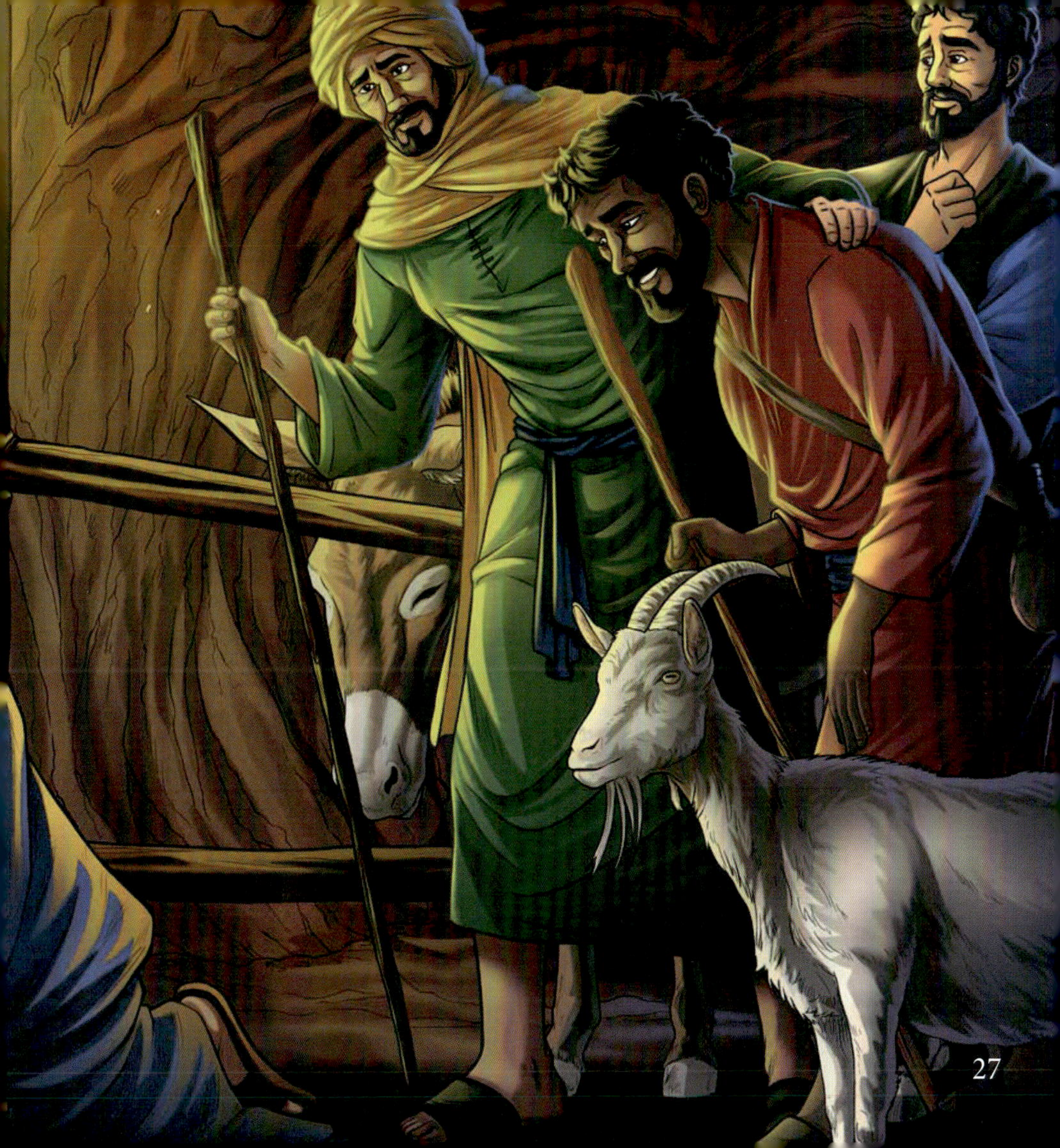

When Jesus was about 30 years old, He was baptized with water by a man named John, and the Spirit of God came down on Jesus like a dove.

God spoke from the heavens stating, "This is my beloved Son, in Whom I am well pleased."

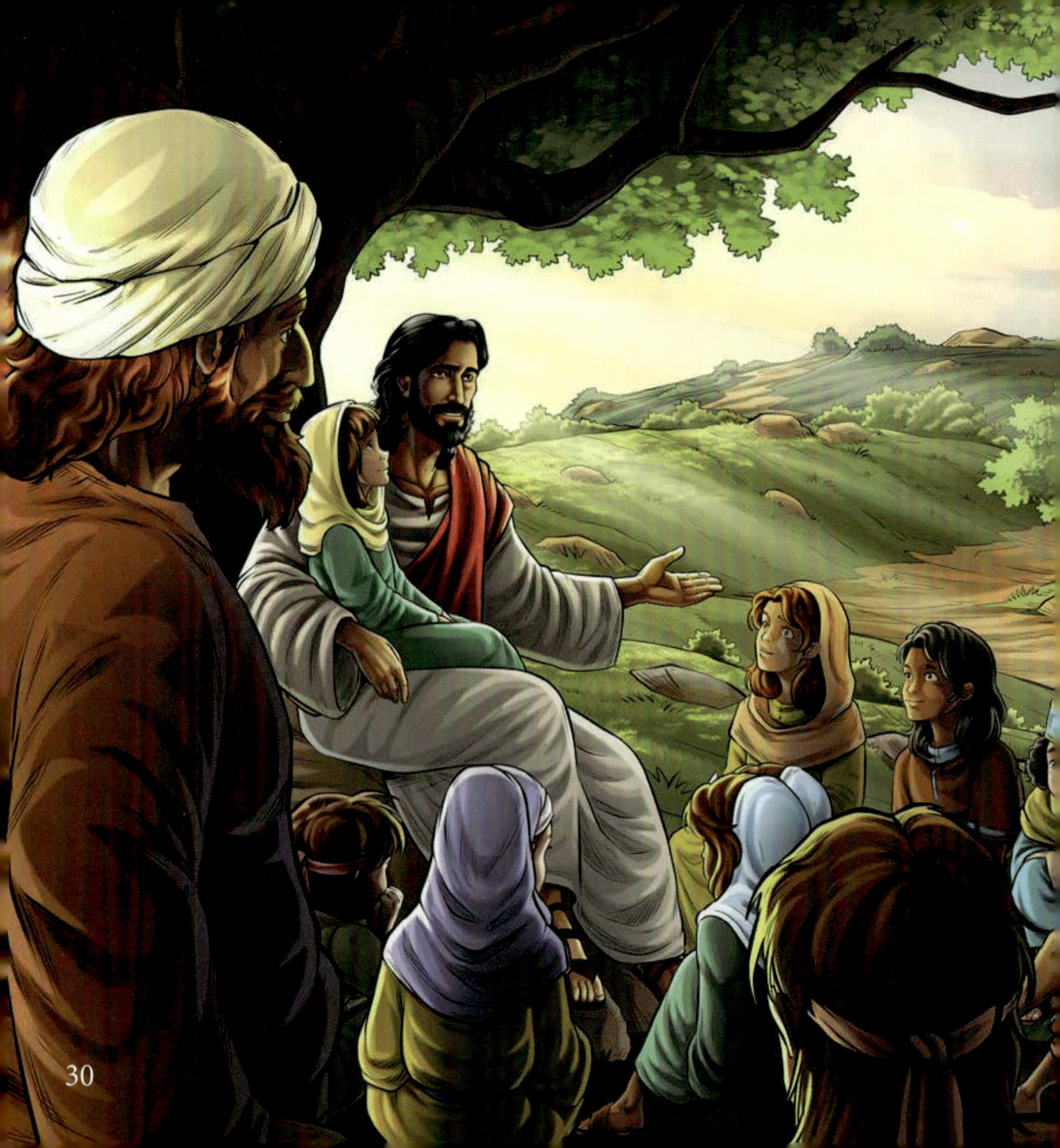

Jesus taught about God with wisdom and understanding.

He healed the sick.

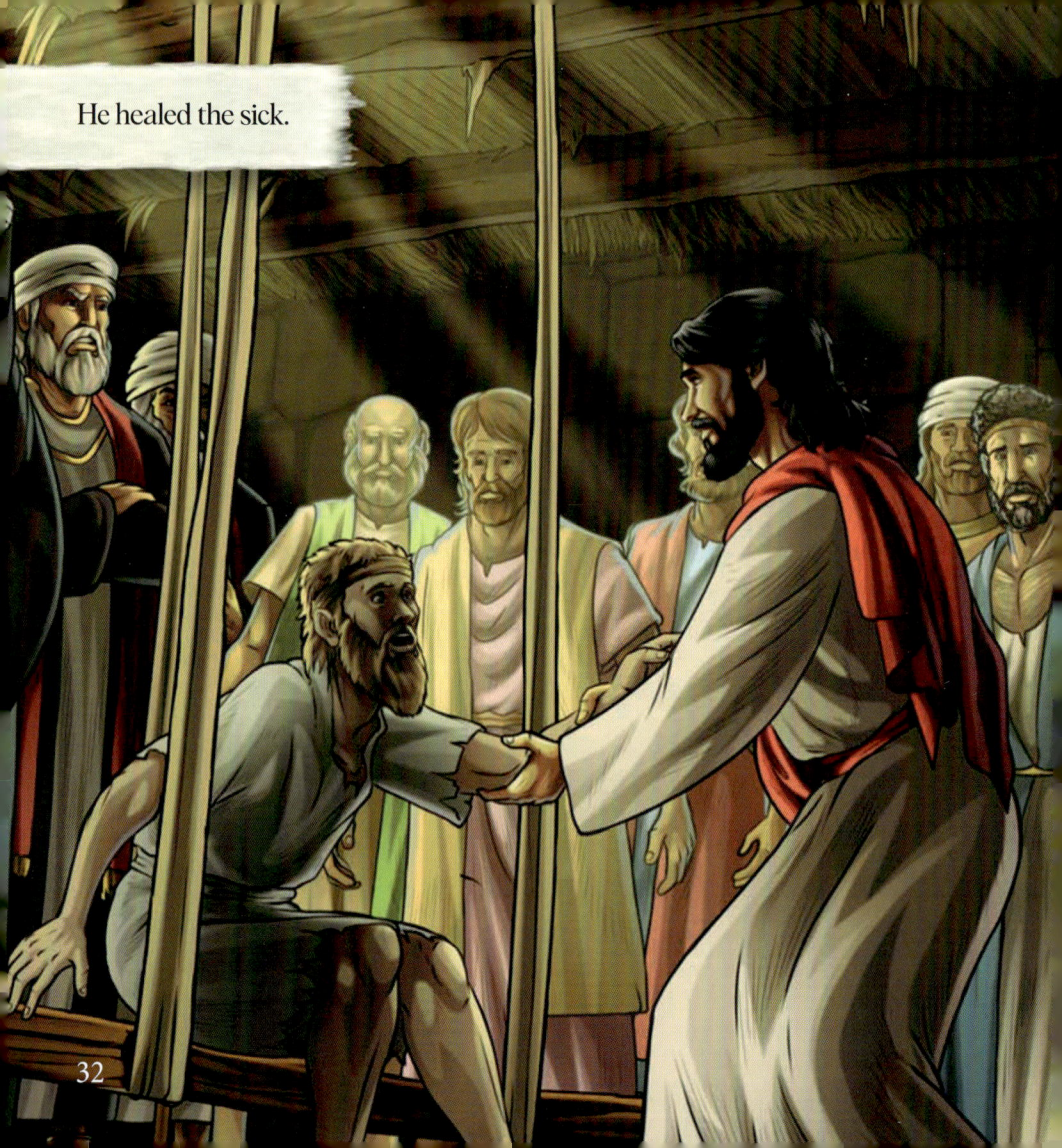

He fed the multitudes.

He cast out demons, and even raised the dead.

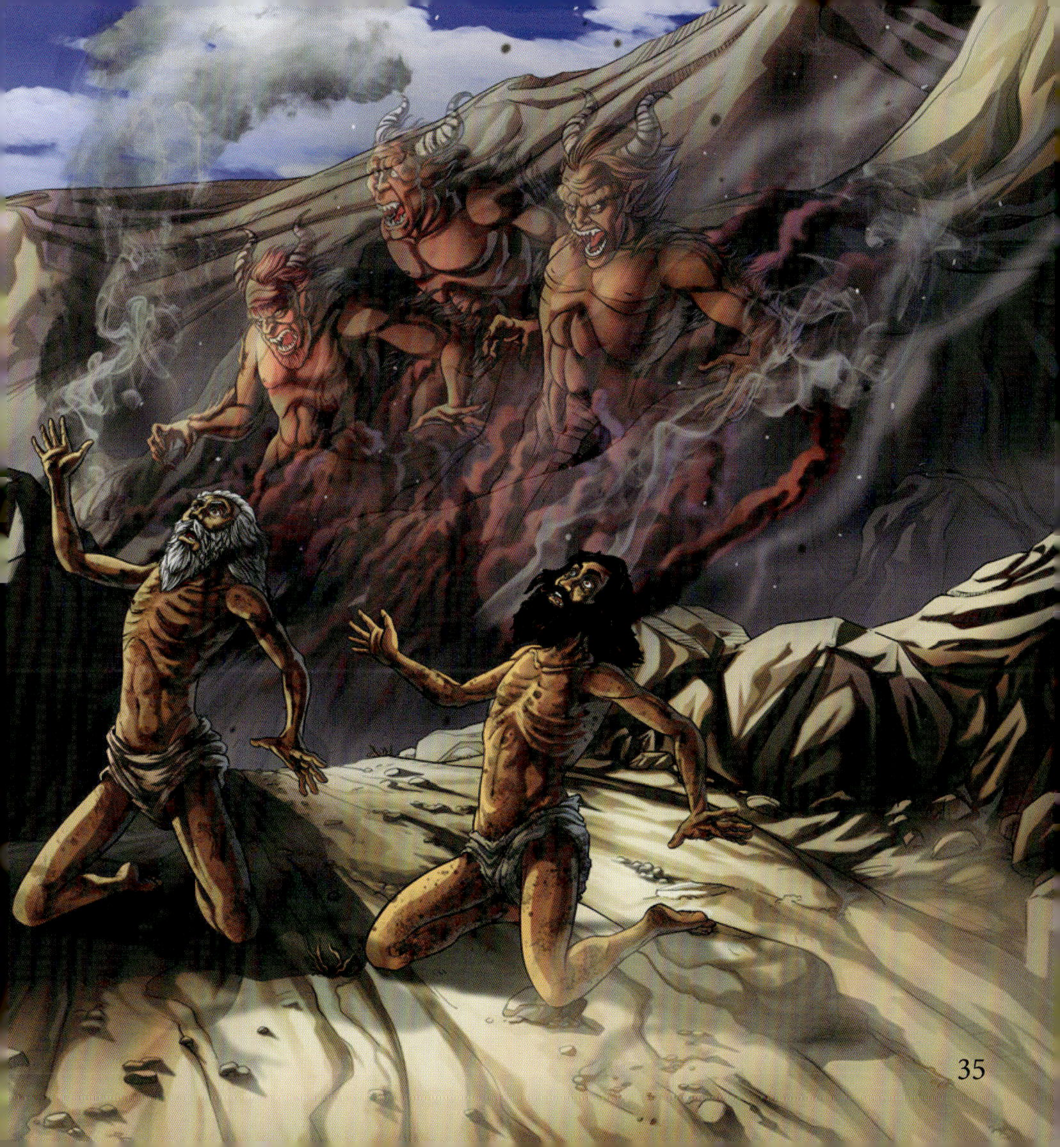

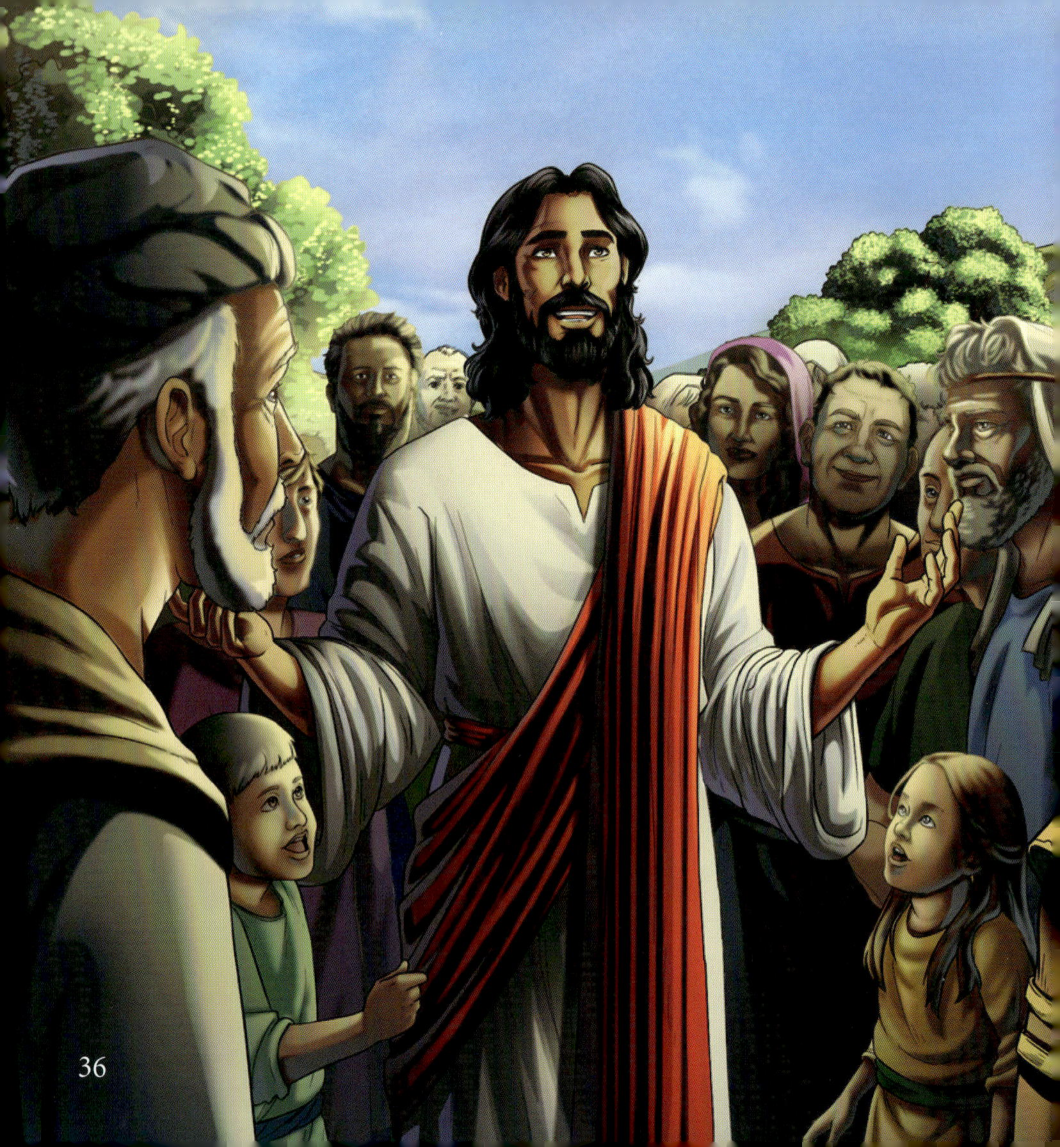

Jesus did all these things in love to point people back to God, His Father, the Creator of all.

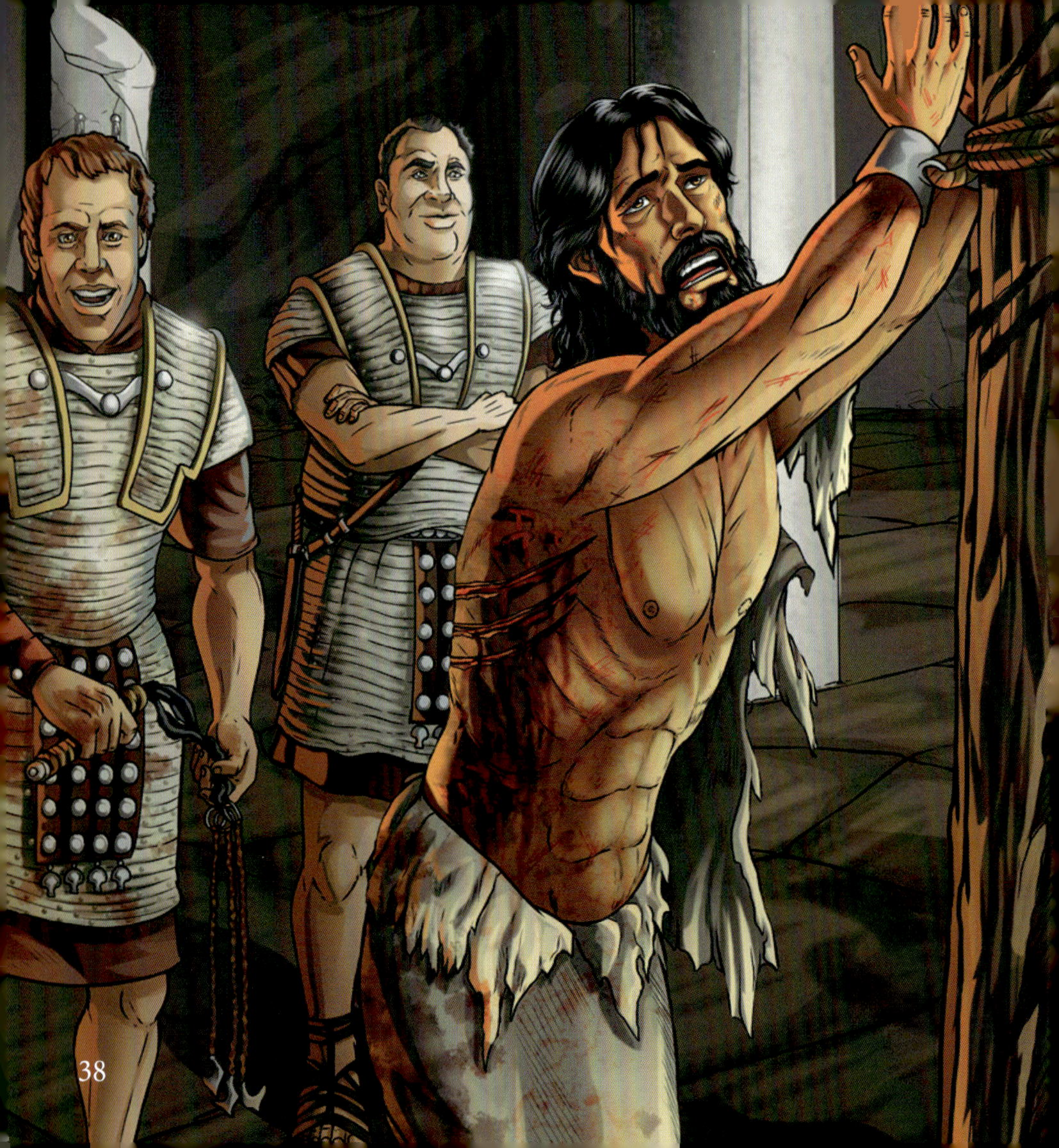

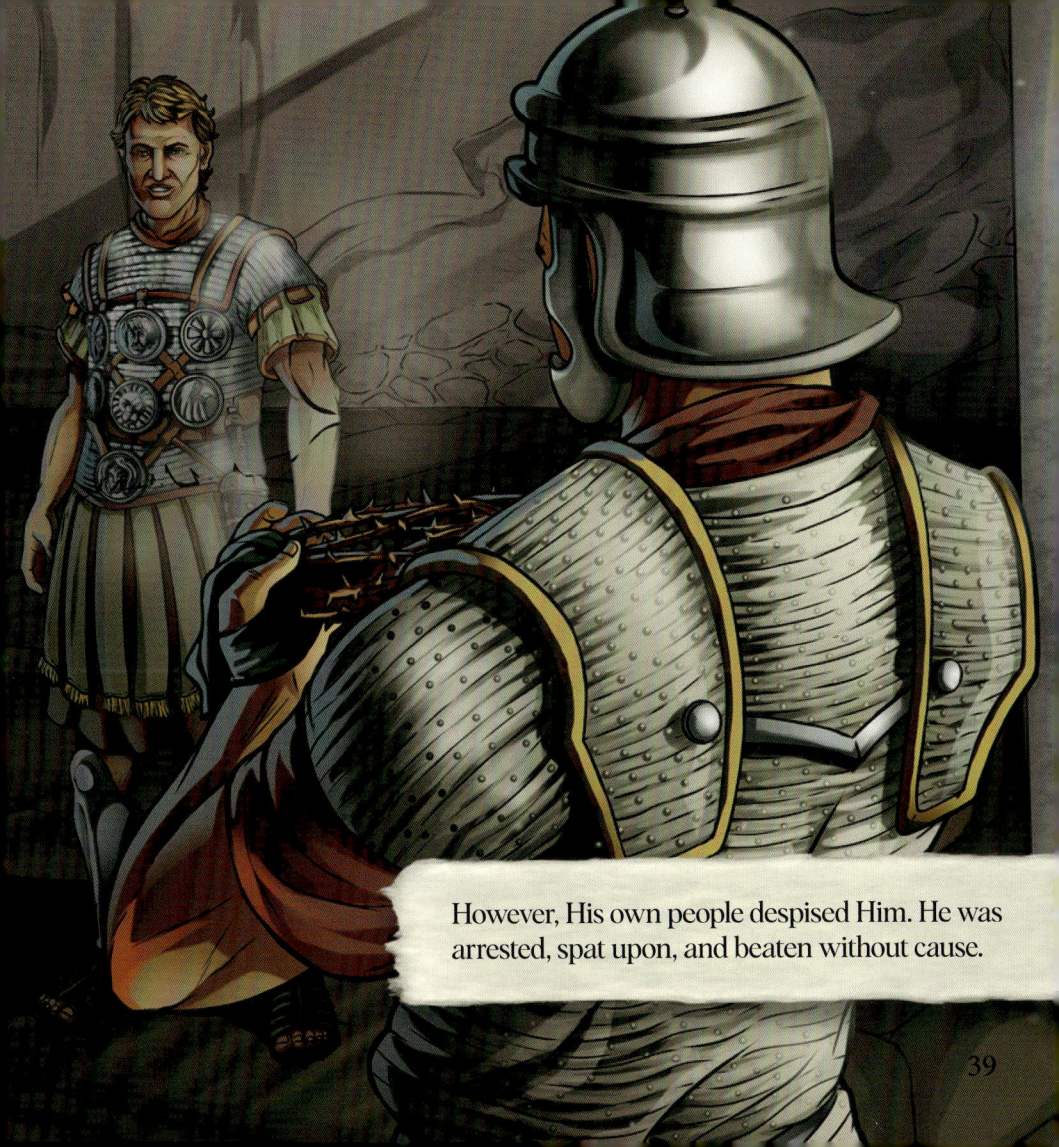

However, His own people despised Him. He was arrested, spat upon, and beaten without cause.

A crown of thorns was placed upon His head.

41

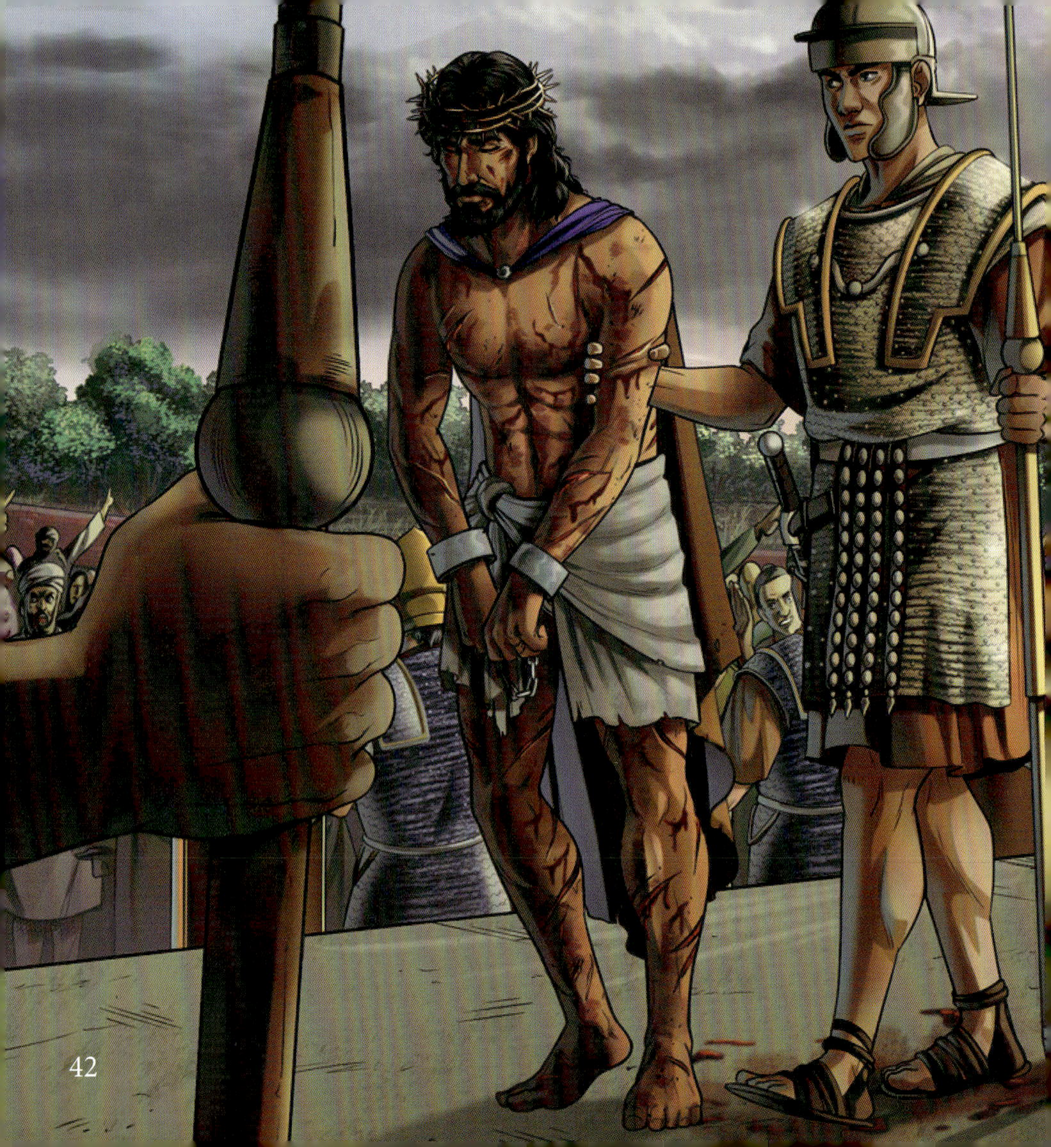

When Roman authorities offered to release Jesus, His own people rejected Him. They insisted that He be nailed to a cross.

So a Roman governor named Pontius Pilate sentenced Jesus to be crucified.

Jesus was forced to carry His cross up a hill called Golgotha.

45

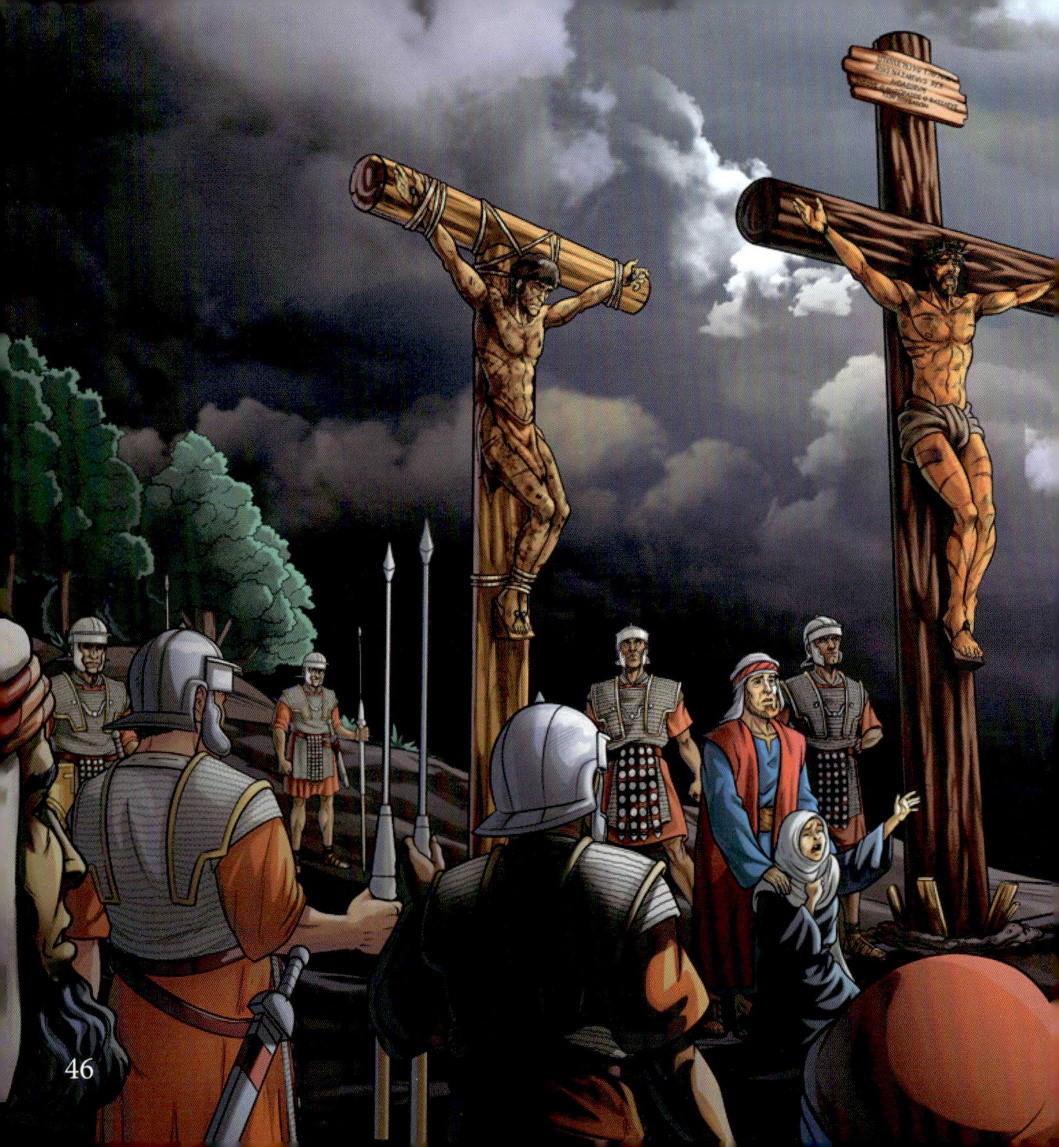

His hands and feet were then nailed to this cross, and He was left to die alongside two thieves.

But even as Jesus hung on this cross, He cried out to His Father in Heaven to forgive those who had done this to Him.

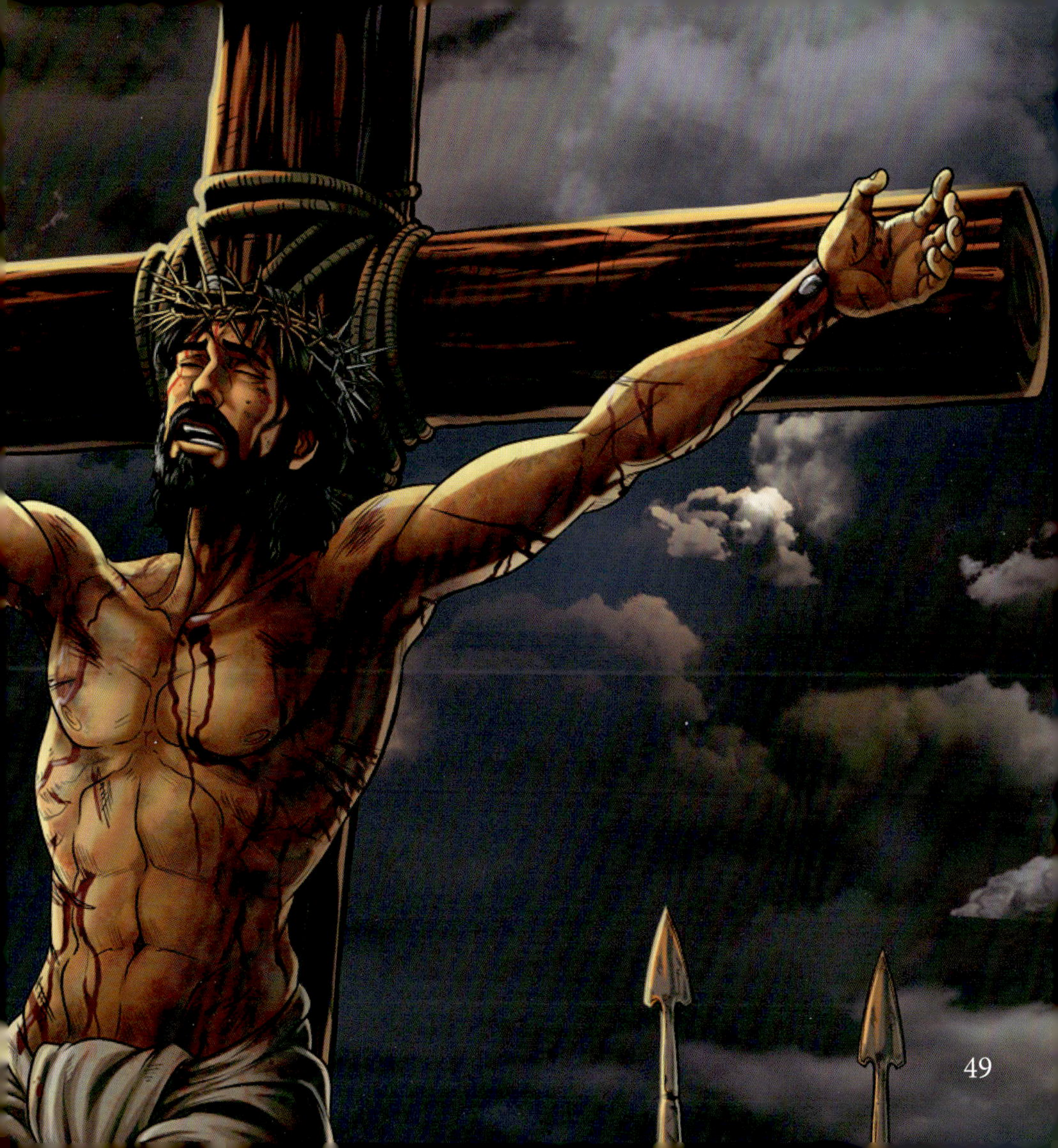

The sky became dark, and after hanging on the cross for many hours, Jesus said, "It is finished."

Then Jesus bowed His head and breathed His last. He had shed His blood for the sins of mankind.

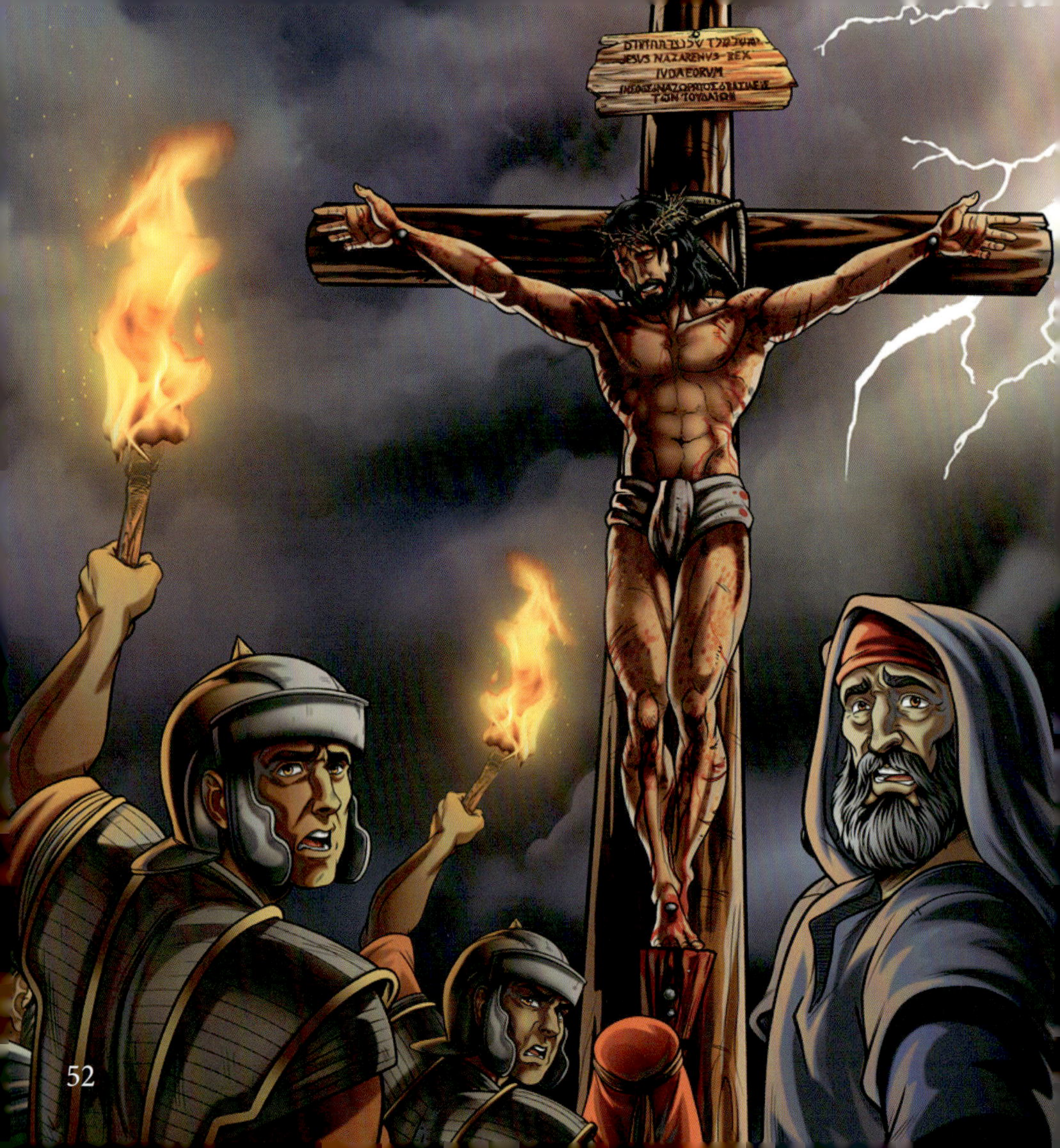
JESVS NAZARENVS REX
IVDAEORVM
ΤΩΝ ΙΟΥΔΑΙΩΝ

The earth shook, and the temple veil tore in two.

His body was removed from the cross, wrapped in linen, and placed in a tomb.

A large stone was rolled in front of the entrance, and Roman guards stood watch.

But on the third day, an angel rolled the stone away: Jesus had risen from the dead!

57

For 40 days, He appeared to those who followed Him and called on His name. Jesus taught His followers about the Kingdom of Heaven and told them not to be afraid, but to tell the world all that they had seen and heard.

59

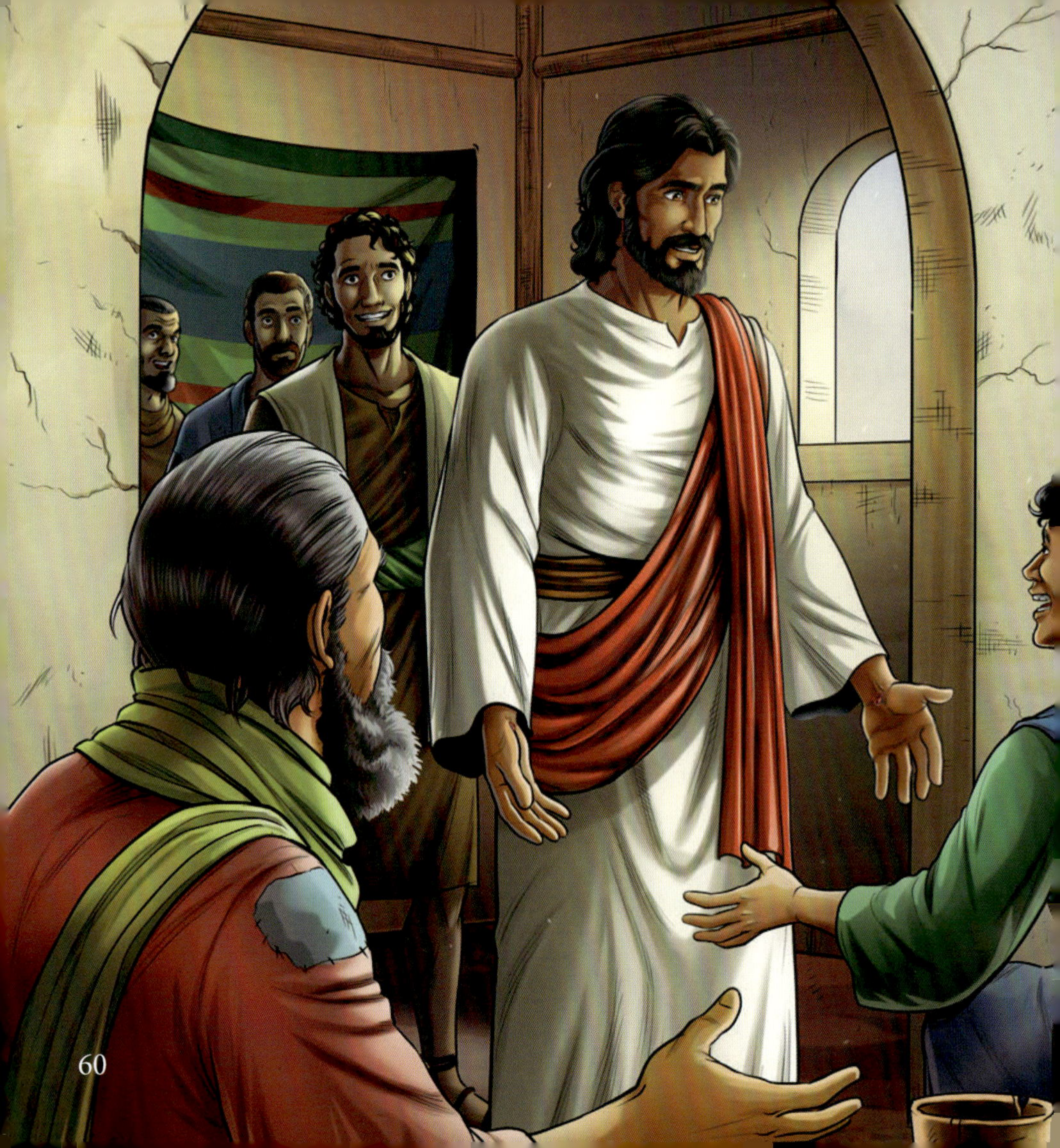

Jesus said that everyone who believes and calls on His name will be saved and will be called a child of God.

Then Jesus ascended, returning to His Father in Heaven.

For God so loved the world that He gave His one and only Son, Jesus, so that everyone who believes in Him will not perish but have everlasting life.

63

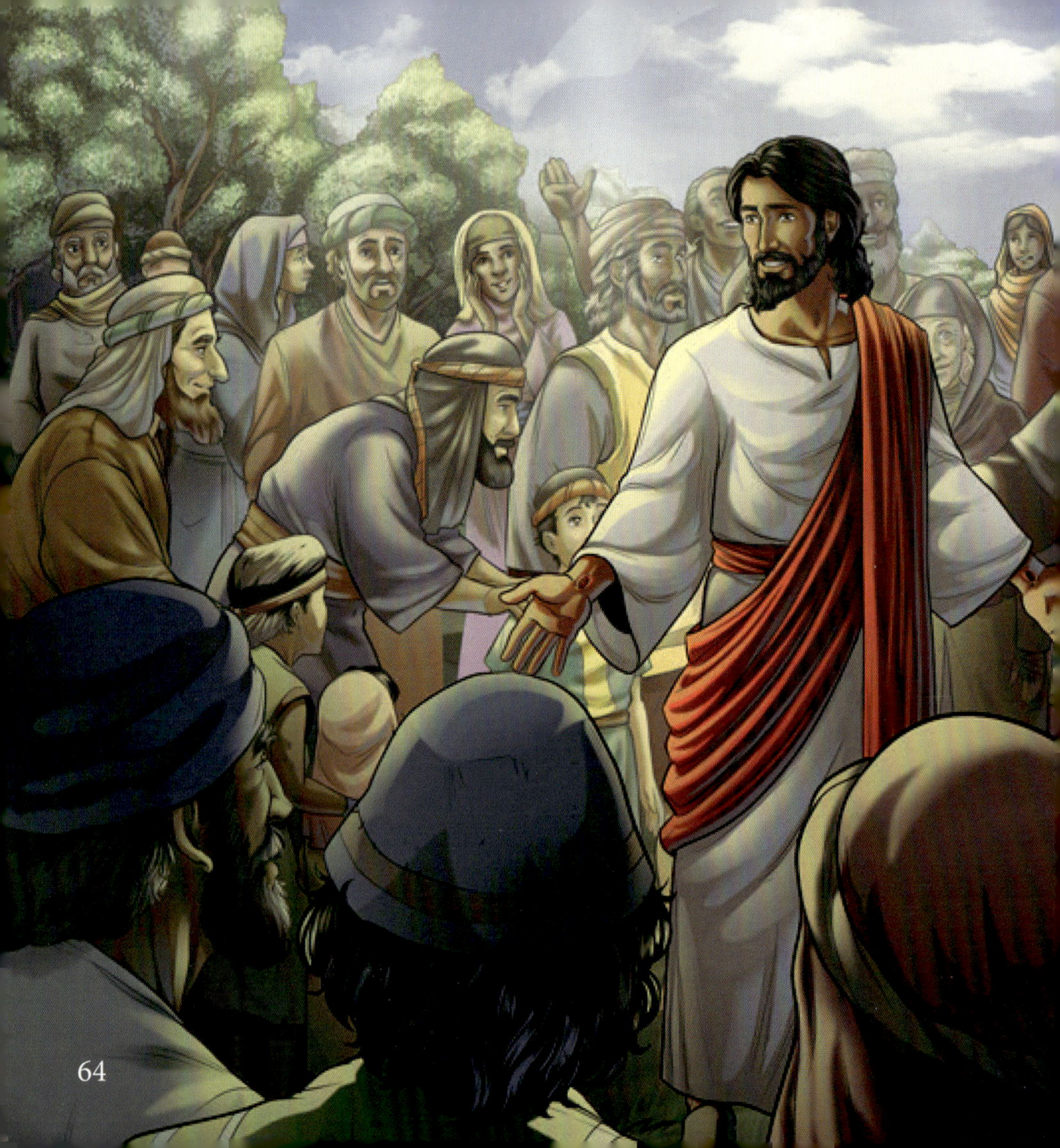

For God did not send Jesus into the world to condemn it, but that the world should be saved through Him.

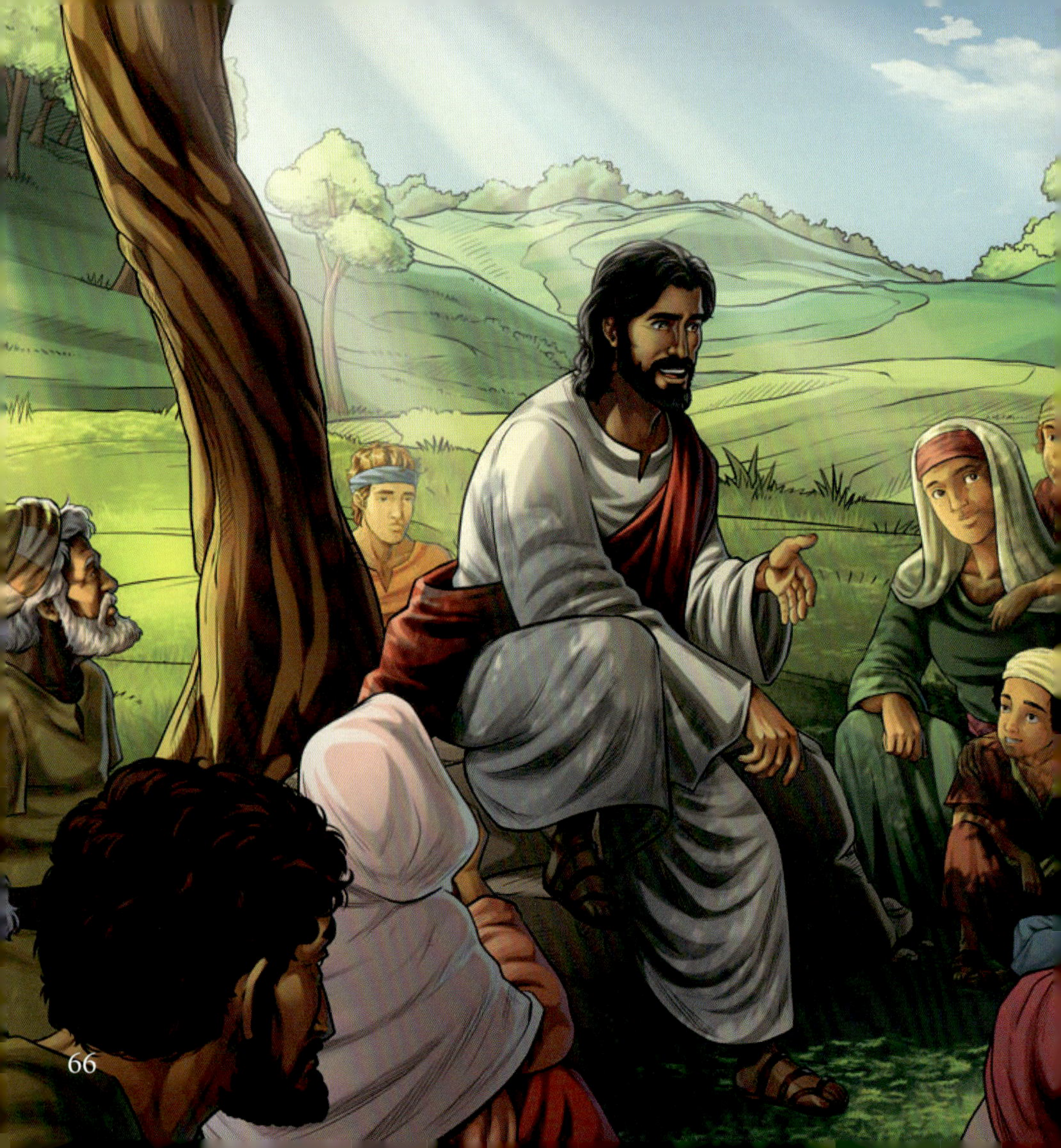

Jesus said that He is the only way back to God. He is the way, the truth, and the life. No one can come to God the Father, the Creator of all, except through Him.

The gift of God is eternal life through His Son Jesus, but those who do not believe will be condemned because the penalty for sin and wrongdoing is death.

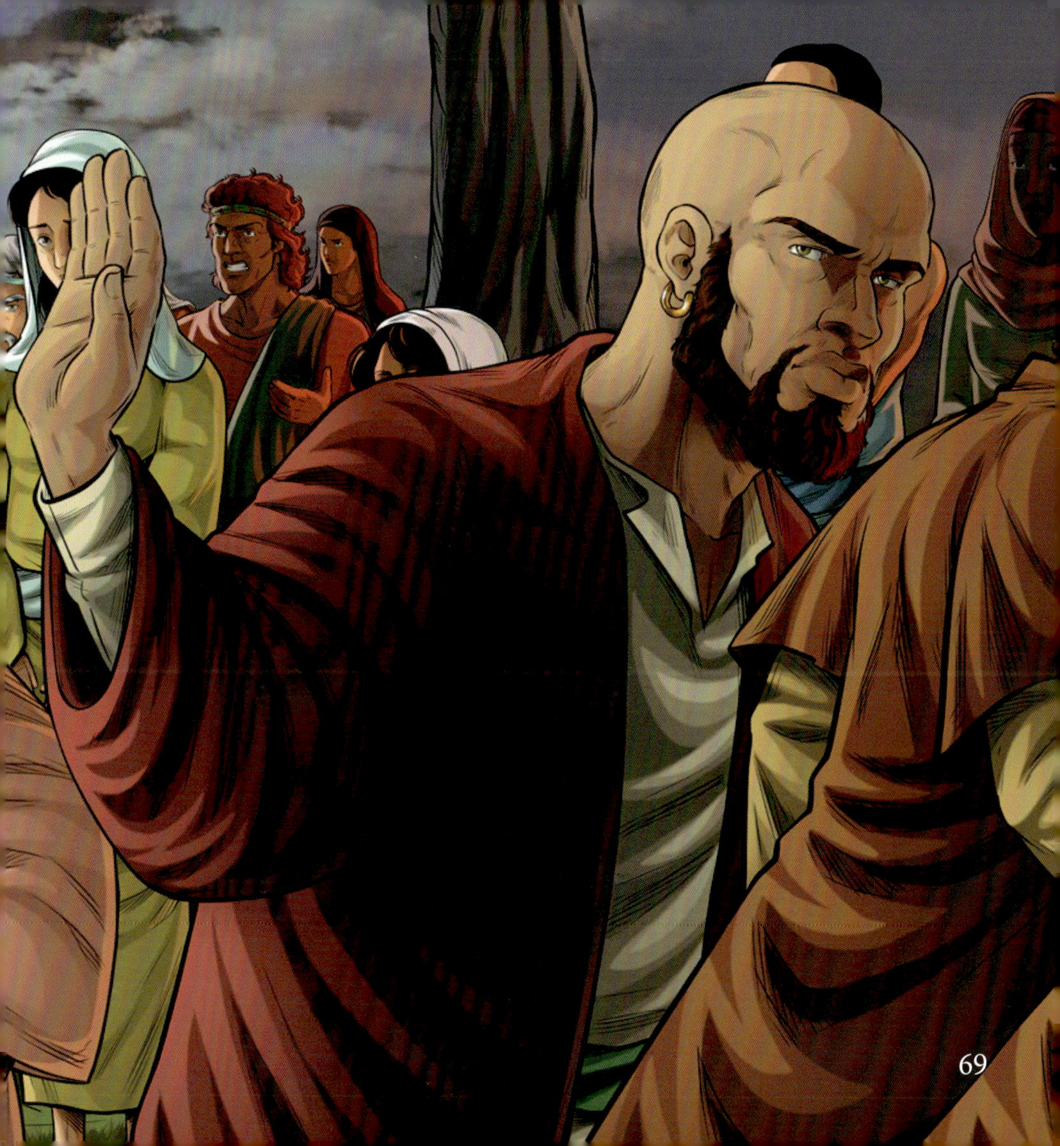

We have all sinned and done evil,
and Jesus has offered to forgive all our sins.

There is no sin that He cannot forgive, but we must ask Jesus to forgive us.

God does not wish that any should perish, but that all should repent. We must call on His name and believe in Him with all our heart.

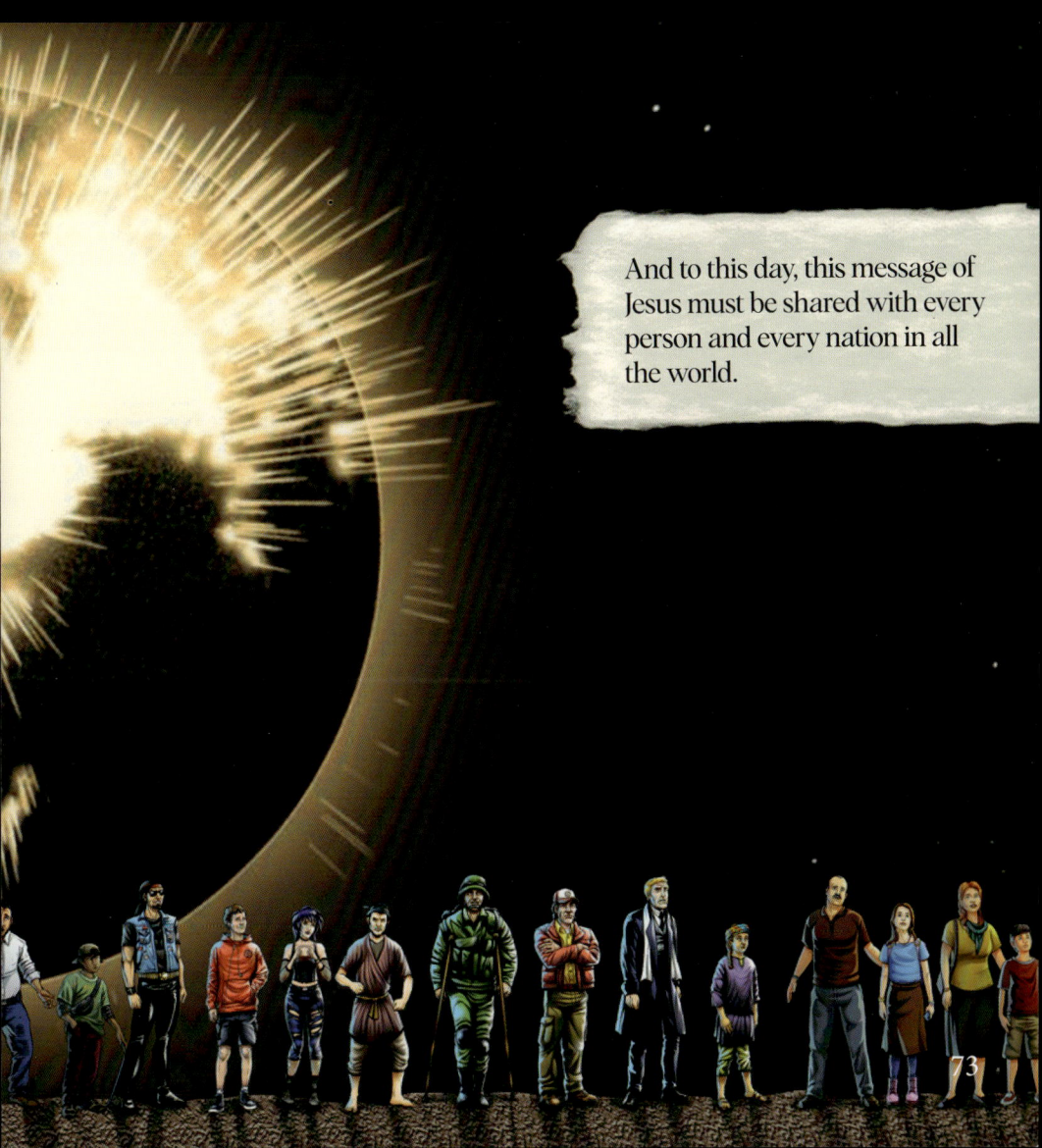

And to this day, this message of Jesus must be shared with every person and every nation in all the world.

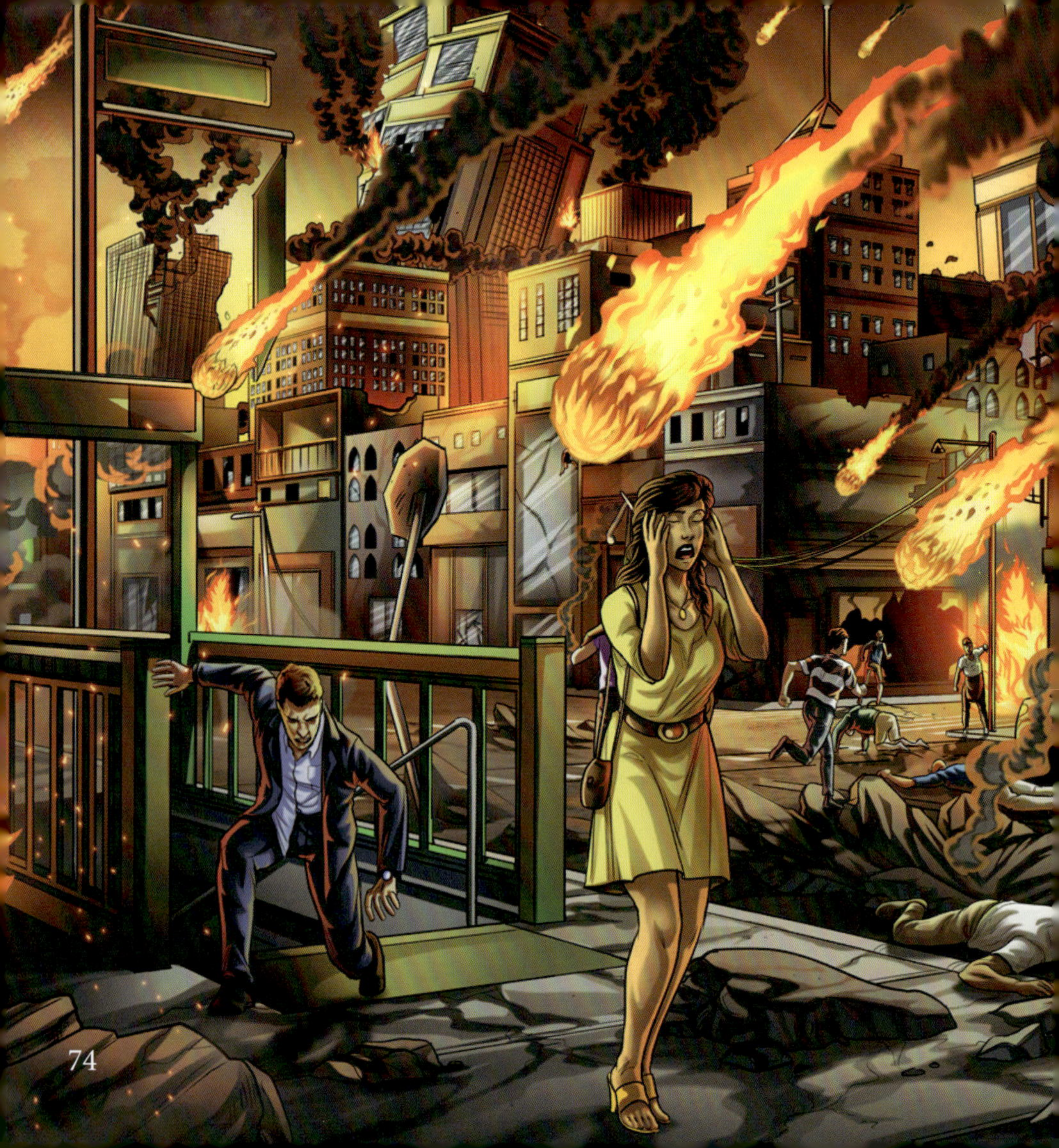

Jesus will come again, and on that day, the sky will grow dark, fire will fall from Heaven, and the earth will shake.

The clouds will part, and Jesus will return with power and great glory, leading the armies of Heaven, and He will judge the whole world.

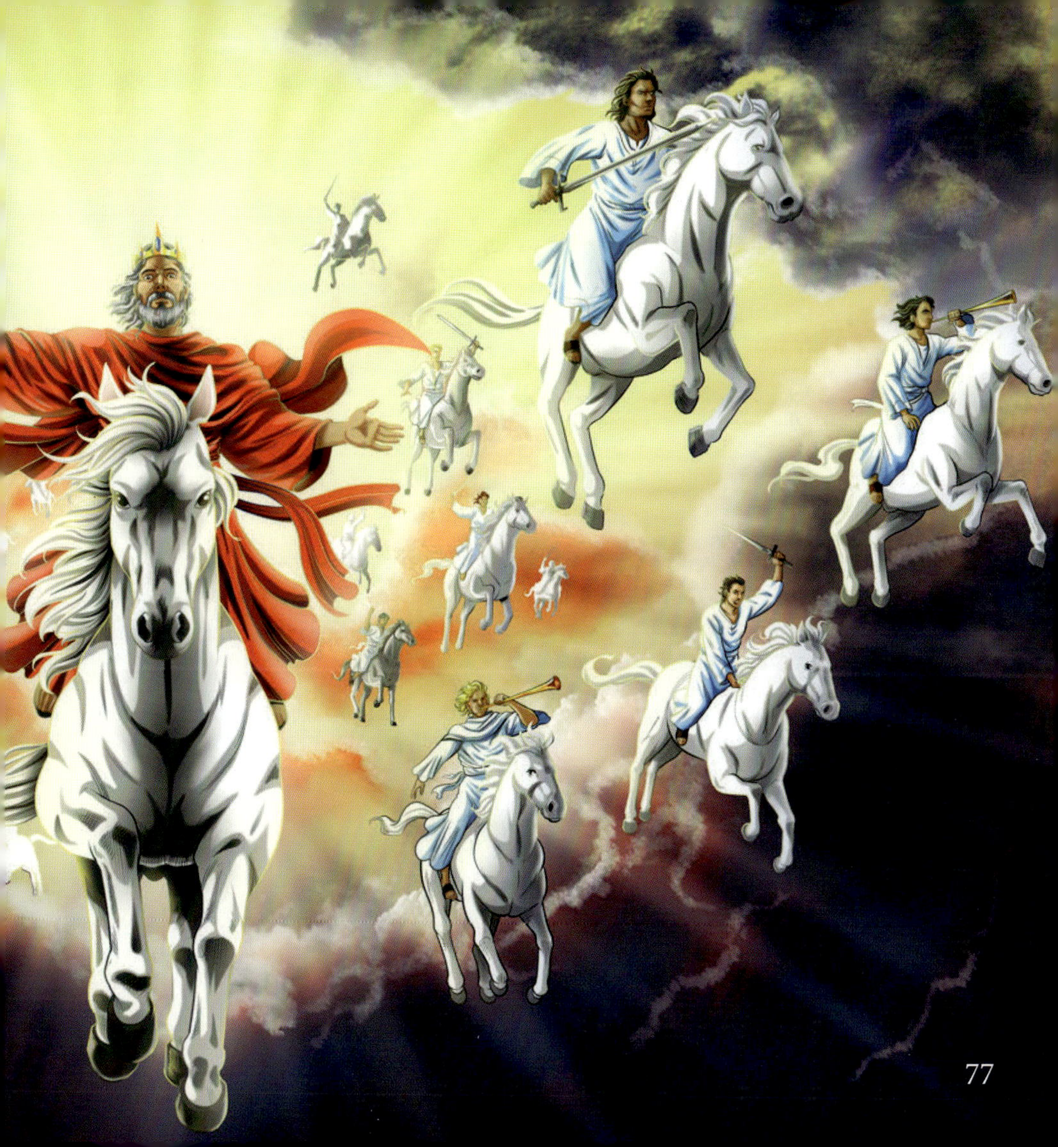

Those who have called on Jesus' name will enter Heaven and be with Jesus for eternity.

He will make everything new. He will wipe away all tears, sorrow, and shame.

79

80

However, those who have rejected His name and have not believed in Him will be eternally condemned. Jesus said, "Narrow is the gate that leads to life, but wide is the gate that leads to destruction."

Now you must decide. Will you, in faith, believe on the Lord Jesus Christ and accept this free gift of salvation? Or will you turn away and reject Him?

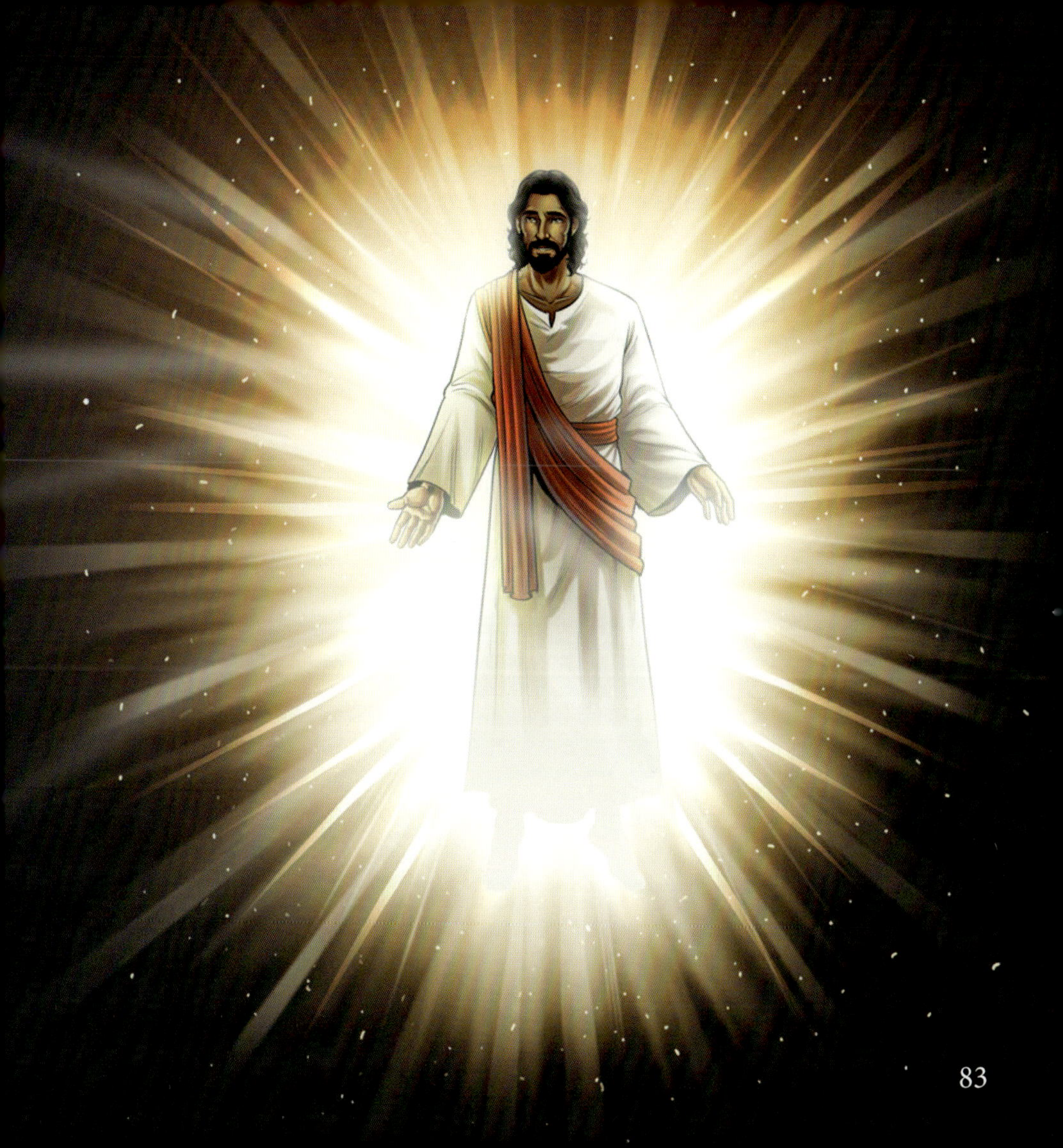

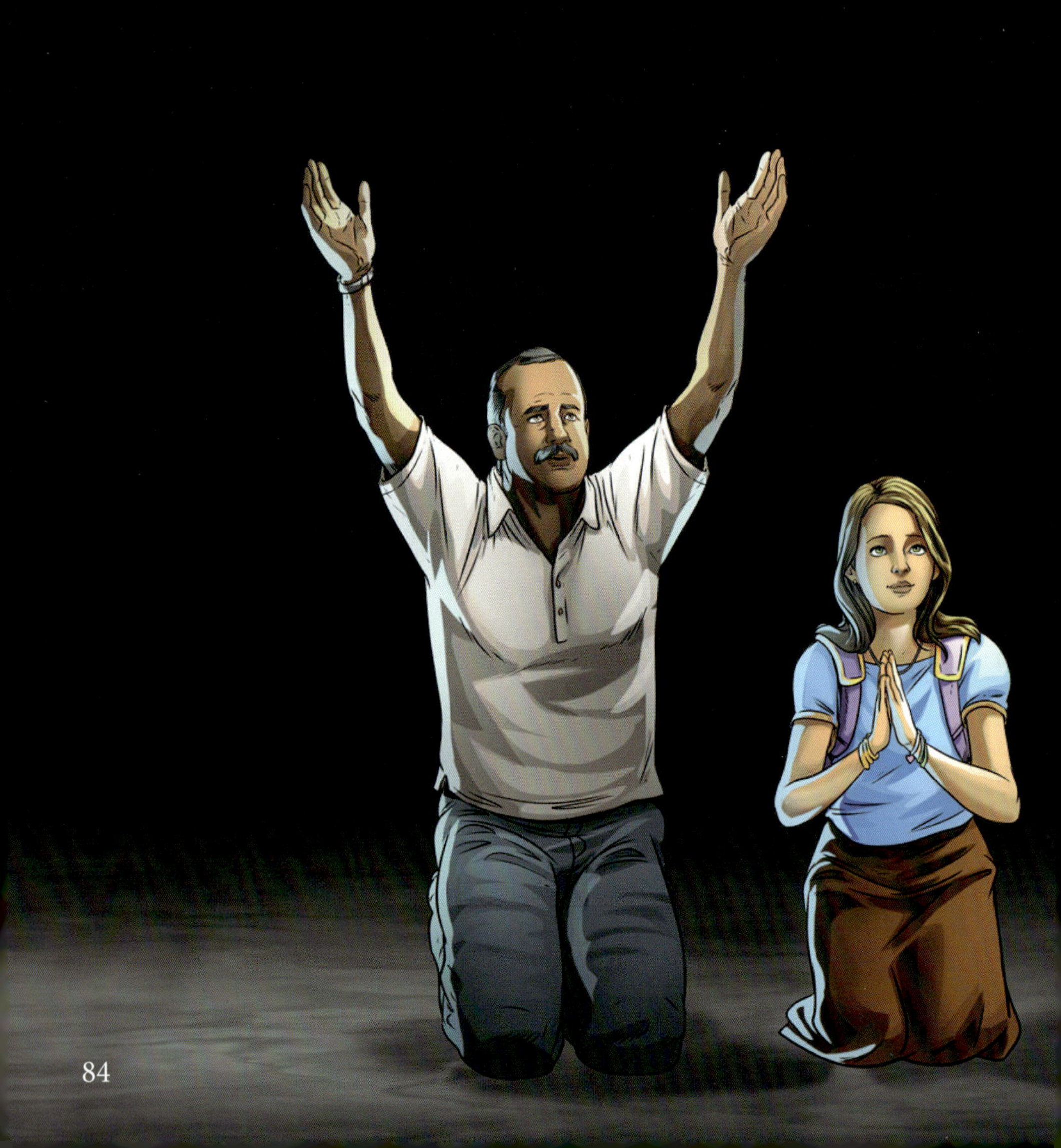

You can call on Jesus right now. Confess your sins, and you will be forgiven. Believe that God raised Jesus from the dead, and you will be saved.

You will become a child of God.

Follow Jesus every day going forward and share this message with others so that they might also become children of God.

87

And together we will say, "Come, Lord Jesus!"

89

Every word of this story is true,
as revealed in God's holy book,
the Bible.

91

Watch
The Real Story of Jesus

www.TheRealStoryofJesus.com

Scan.
Watch.
Share.

We invite you to declare your faith in Jesus Christ and pray this prayer with us.

Dear God,

I confess that Jesus is Lord. I believe He was born of a virgin, died on the cross for my sins, and rose from the dead on the third day.

Today, I confess that I have sinned against You, and there is nothing I can do to save myself. I ask You to forgive me, and I put my trust in Jesus alone. I believe that I am now Your child and that I will spend eternity with You.

Guide me each day by Your Holy Spirit. Help me to love You with all my heart, soul, and mind and to love others as myself. Thank You for saving me through the blood of Your Son, Jesus. In the name of Jesus I pray.

Amen.

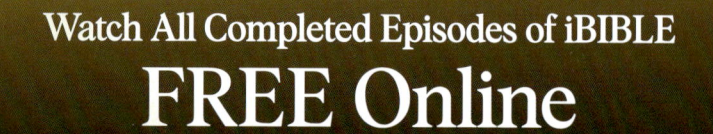

Watch All Completed Episodes of iBIBLE
FREE Online

iBIBLE is the world's first visual presentation of the entire grand narrative of Scripture. It is FREE to replicate, FREE to translate, and FREE to distribute to people all over the globe.

iBIBLE

For more information,
and to watch all completed episodes online,
visit www.i.BIBLE or scan the QR code.

About RevelationMedia

RevelationMedia exists to bring people into a closer relationship with Jesus Christ through visual, audio, and print media in a language they can understand. To promote Biblical literacy, discipleship, and world evangelism, RevelationMedia makes all content freely available for translation and licensing for the global missions community, such as the 2019 animated film *The Pilgrim's Progress*.

And now, for the first time in history, RevelationMedia is creating a complete, cohesive visual and interactive Biblical Narrative called iBIBLE. Reaching children in a media-distracted world, and engaging people all around the globe, RevelationMedia is creating and distributing content to help all people hear the Word of God through media.

Visit us at www.RevelationMedia.com